Read-About® Holidays

Christmas

By David F. Marx

Consultant
Katharine A. Kane, Reading Specialist
Former Language Arts Coordinator,
San Diego County Office of Education

ᏔᏢ Children's Press®
A Division of Grolier Publishing
New York   London   Hong Kong   Sydney
Danbury, Connecticut

Visit Children's Press® on the Internet at:
http://publishing.grolier.com

Designer: Herman Adler Design Group
Photo Researcher: Caroline Anderson

Library of Congress Cataloging-in-Publication Data

Marx, David F.
    Christmas / by David F. Marx.
        p. cm. — (Rookie read-about holidays)
    Includes index.
    Summary: Introduces the history, customs, meaning, and celebration
of Christmas.
        ISBN 0-516-22175-2 (lib. bdg.)   0-516-27153-9 (pbk.)
        1. Christmas—Juvenile literature. [1. Christmas. 2. Holidays.] I. Title.
GT4985.5.M27   2000
394.2663—dc21   00-022632

Do you celebrate Christmas?

Christmas comes on December 25.

In some parts of the United States and Canada, the weather is usually cold and snowy on Christmas.

In other parts of the world, it is quite warm on December 25.

Doesn't this Christmas celebration on an island in the South Seas look different?

Christmas is celebrated all over the world by people of the Christian religion.

Christians remember the birthday of Jesus Christ on Christmas.

Jesus Christ was born long ago.

Christians go to special church services on Christmas. Priests and ministers talk about the importance of peace, love, and friendship.

Some people spend time
on Christmas helping
people who are poor,
or do not have a home,
or who are ill.

Serving soup to poor people

14

Almost everyone loves
to sing Christmas songs,
or carols.

In many countries,
groups of people walk
from house to house on
Christmas Eve (the night
before Christmas) singing
carols for their neighbors.

Many families bring
an evergreen tree into
their homes.

It becomes a Christmas
tree when the family
decorates it with tinsel,
ornaments, and lights.

17

Some families also hang lights and decorations outside their homes.

Gift giving is a Christmas
tradition that has been
around for a long time.

Presents are put under
the tree and opened
on Christmas.

Some children hang
Christmas stockings
for Santa Claus to fill
with toys and candy.

Families often gather for a big Christmas meal. In the United States, the main course is usually roasted ham or turkey.

25

Plum pudding

26

In England, plum pudding is a favorite Christmas food.

In Mexico, people eat a special salad of fruit, beets, and nuts with marshmallows on top.

Celebrating Christmas can be wonderful wherever you live!

Children in Hawaii make Christmas music.

Words You Know

carols

church services

Jesus Christ

plum pudding

ornaments

roasted turkey

South Seas

31